SEE HOW THEY RUN

Campaign Dreams, Election Schemes, and the Race to the White House

Susan E. Goodman

illustrated by Elwood H. Smith

BLOOMSBURY

NEW YORK LONDON OXFORD NEW DELHI SYDNEY

First published in the United States of America in May 2008 by Bloomsbury Children's Books
Revised edition published in July 2012, updated in December 2016
www.bloomsbury.com

Bloomsbury is a registered trademark of Bloomsbury Publishing Plc

For information about permission to reproduce selections from this book, write to
Permissions, Bloomsbury Children's Books, 1385 Broadway, New York, New York 10018
Bloomsbury books may be purchased for business or promotional use. For information on
bulk purchases please contact Macmillan Corporate and Premium Sales Department at
specialmarkets@macmillan.com

The Library of Congress has cataloged the original edition as follows:
Goodman, Susan E.
See how they run : campaign dreams, election schemes, and the race to the White House /
author, Susan E. Goodman ; illustrated by Elwood H. Smith. — 1st U.S. ed.
p.   cm.
Includes bibliographical references.
ISBN-13: 978-1-59990-171-8 • ISBN-10: 1-59990-171-4 (paperback)
ISBN-13: 978-1-59990-285-2 • ISBN-10: 1-59990-285-0 (hardcover)
1. Presidents—United States—Election—Anecdotes—Juvenile literature. 2. Political campaigns—United States—
Anecdotes—Juvenile literature. 3. Elections—United States—Anecdotes—Juvenile literature.
4. Presidential candidates—United States—Anecdotes—Juvenile literature. I. Smith, Elwood H., ill. II. Title.
JK528.G66 2008   324.973—dc22   2007044452

ISBN 978-1-59990-897-7 (revised edition)

Printed in China by C&C Offset Printing Co., Ltd., Shenzhen, Guangdong
3 5 7 9 10 8 6 4 2

All papers used by Bloomsbury Publishing, Inc., are natural, recyclable products
made from wood grown in well-managed forests. The manufacturing processes
conform to the environmental regulations of the country of origin.

To Jill Davis—it should always be like this
—S. E. G.

For my dear old pal, Slug Signorino
—E. H. S.

★ Contents ★

Introduction

Important things happen in the fall.

Going back to school.

The World Series.

HALLOWEEN!

It's also election time, when we choose people to run our cities and states. Then, every four years, we elect someone to lead the whole country:

the president of the United States!

A Little More Intro!

We put our Founding Fathers on pedestals and think they were perfect. But they weren't.

George Washington was always in debt. He had to borrow money to get to his own inauguration. Thomas Jefferson and John Adams were brilliant patriots and presidents, but they often acted like babies. For years they competed about everything. In fact, Adams's last words were "Thomas Jefferson still survives," not knowing that his former enemy had died just a few hours earlier.

Alexander Hamilton . . . well, ask someone about him when you're older!

After the Revolution, these very real, very imperfect men did the best job they could designing our government. Since then other real, imperfect people have led it. Good things have happened and bad things have happened. Good things have become better and bad things worse. Good things have become worse and bad things better.

Confusing? You bet!

John Adams

Thomas Jefferson

That's why the rest of us must help keep the government on track.

One way we do this is to vote. Voting lets us help create the rules and pick our leaders. It expresses our opinions on issues that affect the government, issues that affect our lives! But we can't just flick a switch on Election Day. We have to know how the system works so we can make good decisions.

Consider what happened in Milton, Washington, when Boston Curtis won his election in 1938. Milton's mayor had put this totally unknown candidate on the ballot to prove how important it is to know who you are voting for.

Boston Curtis was a mule.

★ 1 ★
A Short History of Democracy

The Beginnings . . .

When was the first election? It's impossible to tell. For all we know, people voted in prehistoric times.

FLINT, FLINT, HE'S OUR MAN. IF HE CAN'T CAVE PAINT, NO ONE CAN.

ELECT GROG, KEEPER OF THE FLAME.

A VOTE FOR HOMO SAPIENS IS A VOTE FOR PROGRESS.

Early people may have had elections; we just can't be sure. They didn't have a written language, so they couldn't leave us records—let alone campaign posters or bumper stickers.

Beware of Greeks Bearing Gifts

The ancient Greeks get credit for inventing democracy, probably because they had the best word for it. The "demo" part comes from *demos*, which means "the people." "Cracy" comes from *kratein*, meaning "to rule."

Rule by the people.

Starting in 510 BC, the citizens of Athens, Greece, gathered in the Assembly and voted on important community issues. Each one had an equal voice in deciding what would happen. This was the purest democracy of all time—sort of. Only adult males, born in Athens with Athenian parents, could be citizens with full legal rights. That meant only one out of eight Athenians could vote on decisions that affected all their lives.

The Average Greek Citizen

There's No Place Like Rome

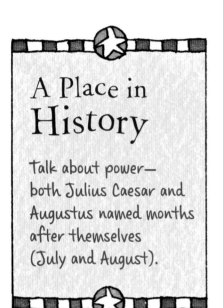

A Place in History

Talk about power—both Julius Caesar and Augustus named months after themselves (July and August).

Around the same time and a little to the west, the city of Rome began working on its version of democracy. That is, when its citizens or armies weren't too busy conquering everyone else around them.

Roman democracy was different from the Greek version, in which ordinary citizens voted on major issues. Instead Romans voted to pick the people who would make decisions for them. They elected senators, who held their jobs for life. They also elected leaders called consuls, who controlled the army and created laws. But a Roman citizen's best privilege was being the only one in the Empire who could wear a toga!

Eventually Roman leaders became a little too power hungry. Julius Caesar got himself declared Dictator for Life. Augustus took the title of Emperor. Then he went all out and declared himself a god.

So far our presidents have shown more self-control.

1,800 Years Later—Here Comes American Democracy

George Washington and the rest of our Founding Fathers borrowed bits and pieces from past democracies to create our own. They named our Senate after the Roman Senate. They adopted a British idea from the thirteenth century, saying that the government must respect a citizen's legal rights.

George and his crew wanted a government where people had some say in how to rule the country—but not too much. They didn't trust all their fellow Americans, especially those without much education. So they rejected the Greek method of having citizens vote directly on laws. Decisions would be made by people who "represented" the citizens instead, just like in the Roman Republic.

A FOUNDING FATHER'S WISH LIST:

Things to Borrow from Rome

1. Senate (no girls allowed!)
2. Marble statues of Founding Fathers (only if clothed!)
3. Togas
4. The veto? NO! (just kidding)
5. Taxes
6. Months named after us— Frankuary? Jeffember?

ROMAN DEMOCRACY

In 1787, the Founding Fathers locked themselves up for four months to write our Constitution. Coming up with this description of our new government wasn't easy. They all had different ideas and had to compromise. George Washington's face often wore its "Valley Forge look."

Here's what they came up with—a national government with three branches. Our Congress (the legislative branch) has two parts or houses: the Senate and the House of Representatives. Congress can make laws to raise taxes, improve citizens' lives, and defend the country. The president heads the executive branch. He (and someday soon, maybe she) carries out laws and is head of the military. He also appoints judges to the Supreme Court, part of our judicial branch. The court's job is to enforce existing laws and decide if the other two branches are obeying the Constitution.

What Did Ben Say?

Shortly after the Constitutional Convention ended, a woman asked Benjamin Franklin what kind of government the Founding Fathers created. Franklin's answer? "A republic, madam, if you can keep it." In other words, our kind of government needs citizens who care enough to stay informed and take part. In other, other words . . .

VOTE!

Getting Better All the Time

Is the Constitution a perfect plan? Nope, but the people who wrote it were smart enough to know that. They improved it right away by writing the Bill of Rights, the first ten amendments (additions) to the Constitution. We've been making it better ever since.

The Good News: The United States was the first modern democracy with an elected government protecting the freedom and rights of its citizens.

The Bad News: In the beginning, only white men who owned land could vote.

The Good News: In 1856, white men who didn't own land got that right.

The Bad News: Everyone else was still left out in the cold. Changing beliefs and values isn't easy; it takes lots of thought and struggle.

The Good News: African American and other nonwhite men began voting in 1870.

The Bad News: People's beliefs and values change too slowly. An African American's right to vote was often denied in the South and parts of the North until the civil rights movement of the 1960s.

The Good News: American women of all races got the vote in 1920.

The Bad News: Women in New Zealand, Australia, Finland, Norway, Canada, Estonia, England, Ireland, the Soviet Union, Austria, Czechoslovakia, Germany, Hungary, Armenia, Azerbaijan, Poland, Luxembourg, and Holland were able to vote before them. At least the United States beat Switzerland, where women couldn't vote until 1971!

The Good News: Native Americans began voting in 1924.

The Bad News: Seems like a long wait, given that they were here first. What's more, some states banned them from voting until the 1940s.

The Good News: In 1971, the voting age was reduced to eighteen years old.

The Bad News: You've still got a while before you can vote.

The Good News: You have other ways to make your opinion heard. Keep reading to find out what they are!

College Daze

In 1888, Americans went to the polls to elect the twenty-third president of the United States. Grover Cleveland got about one hundred thousand more votes than Benjamin Harrison did.

Want to guess who won?

Benjamin Harrison.

Welcome to the weird system we call the electoral college. If you ask most adults about it, they'll cough once or twice, then change the subject. You don't have to be in college yourself to understand the electoral college, but it is a little confusing.

Take a deep breath and keep reading.

When the American people vote, it's called the popular vote. To elect anyone from a dogcatcher to a senator, the popular vote decides who will win. But the popular vote does not elect the president. If Cleveland and Harrison had run for mayor of Mudville, for example, Cleveland would have won.

The Winners!?!

This early version of a campaign button featuring General Benjamin Harrison and Levi P. Morton is from 1888.

YOU MEAN, IF I GET 48% OF TEXANS TO VOTE FOR ME, BUT I DON'T GET ENOUGH ELECTORS' VOTES, I LOSE THE ENTIRE STATE TO YOU?

But when we vote for president and vice president, we're actually voting for a person called an elector. Electors are the ones who elect the president.

What's going on here? How did the writers, or framers, of the Constitution come up with this one?

Once again, our Founding Fathers were worried that the American public couldn't or wouldn't learn about the different candidates. Don't forget, back then people didn't have TV news or even political parties to supply information. So they gave us electors, who would learn about the candidates and vote for us.

The framers also wanted to make sure that less-populated states weren't overwhelmed by big ones in this all-important election. Luckily some math whiz found a way to give states with fewer people a little extra help. The number of electors a state gets is based on the number of people it has in Congress. (Each state has two senators and then a number of representatives based on the state's population.) The state of Wyoming ends up with only three electors. Still these three votes, compared to the fifty-five votes of our most-populated state, California, give it more power than just using population alone.

★ 17 ★

Are You Wondering . . .

Why doesn't the entire country use the winner-take-all system? You'll have to ask the holdouts: Maine and Nebraska.

Do you have a headache yet? Imagine how it feels trying to explain this to you. But hang on, we're not done. Here's another wrinkle:

The Constitution created the electoral college, but it doesn't supply rules for voting that the states must follow. Over time, states have changed the way they pick their electors. Forty-eight of our fifty states have adopted a winner-take-all system. That means if you vote for Barnaby Mugwump for president and Jane Doozle wins the majority of votes in your state, she gets all of your state's electoral votes. That's how Benjamin Harrison ended up winning in 1888. The states Harrison won had more electors than the ones won by Cleveland.

Thomas Jefferson thought the electoral college was "the most dangerous blot on our Constitution." President Jimmy Carter tried to get rid of it, but he couldn't get enough votes in Congress to make the change.

Maybe you'll have a chance to vote on it yourself someday.

I NEVER WENT TO COLLEGE AND I WISH OUR COUNTRY DIDN'T EITHER.

Grover Cleveland

College Curiosities

This electoral college system creates some bizarre situations:

- Grover Cleveland isn't the only candidate who won the popular vote and lost the presidency. This has happened five times in our history, including the election between Donald Trump and Hillary Clinton in 2016. Each time it has made more than half of the voters very angry.

- If a candidate wins the eleven most-populated states (271 electoral votes), he or she becomes president despite losing in thirty-nine states.

- If a candidate does not receive a majority of electoral votes (270) or there is a tie, the House of Representatives chooses the president and the Senate chooses the vice president.

Let's Have a Party—or Two

George Washington was our first president. He got everyone's vote. Sounds impressive, but it wasn't really. The first time, no one ran against him.

George Washington hated the idea of political parties. He thought they would divide Americans against each other. Before Washington's eight years in office were over, however, people were already arguing about how the government should work. And they were forming groups that represented their different ideas.

In the early years, there were the Federalist Party (city guys who wanted strong government), the Anti-Federalist Party (country guys who wanted states to have the power), and the Democratic-Republican Party (Jefferson's party, which wanted more types of people to be able to vote). There was even a party called the Whigs, pronounced the "wigs," although it had nothing to do with weirdos in fake white hair.

WHIG

WIG

PIG

What Would Ben Say?

We can't be sure of what Franklin would say about party politics. But he'd certainly remind us that "honesty is the best policy." He'd also think to himself, "If passion drives you, let reason hold the reins."

By the 1860s, the United States had settled into having two major parties—the Democrats and the Republicans. Over time, these groups have held different beliefs. Today the Republican Party tends to think that government should not interfere too much in people's lives. Republicans believe that it's better for people to help themselves. Democrats tend to believe that if people do need help, the government should pitch in. They also want the federal government to protect people's rights.

Of course, the programs Democrats want cost money, and Republicans often don't want to spend it in that way. Republican president Ronald Reagan gave his opinion of their differences by saying, "Republicans believe every day is the Fourth of July, but Democrats believe every day is April 15." That's the day we pay our income taxes!

DEMOCRAT

REPUBLICAN

Like anything complicated, political parties have their good and bad sides.

On one hand, parties can make choices easier for voters. If someone agrees with a Democratic point of view, chances are, he'll like a Democratic candidate. Parties are good for candidates as well as voters. When the Republican Party supports a candidate, for example, it puts the strength of its people and money behind her.

There is another hand, though. Parties often compete to be biggest and strongest. This desire to beat each other can get in the way of the reason they are really there—good government. Party politicians can become very powerful. Sometimes they use this power badly.

Party Favors

In the nineteenth and early twentieth centuries, many leaders handed out jobs or favors in exchange for money and more power. After the Civil War, for example, men who wanted to be judges had to "contribute" about $15,000 to the Republican Party, an amount that is worth more than $200,000 today. A seat in Congress was a relative bargain at only $4,000, or $60,000 in today's money. Whatever the amount, these contributions made certain leaders very rich.

Party Crashers: Third Parties in the United States

Teddy Roosevelt

For the most part, we have a two-party system. In other words, the Democrats and Republicans run the show. But you can always find a few other candidates running for office. They belong to what we call third parties—even if there are ten of them on the ballot.

Third parties usually form to support a particular cause and then name themselves after it. Today's Green Party works to save the environment. The Prohibition Party, very active one hundred years ago, wanted to prohibit, or forbid, the use of alcohol. Want to guess what the No New Taxes Party and the Protect the Earth Party were interested in?

Former Republican president Teddy Roosevelt wanted his job back in 1912. But the Republicans already had a president in office, President William H. Taft. So Roosevelt formed the Bull Moose Party because he was "as fit as a bull moose." He acted like a bull too, charging around, calling President Taft a "fathead" with the "brains of a guinea pig." And Roosevelt was as brave as a bull. While campaigning, he was shot in the chest but kept talking for another hour, waving the bloody pages of his speech in front of the crowd.

At election time, some Republicans stayed with Taft and some voted for Roosevelt. By forming this third party, Roosevelt split the Republican vote. This division allowed Democrat Woodrow Wilson to become president.

This is not the only time a third party has changed election results. In the 2000 election, Green Party candidate Ralph Nader got more than ninety-seven thousand votes in Florida. Most people think that if these voters hadn't chosen Nader, many of them would have voted for Democrat Al Gore. In the end, the votes Nader received were enough to let George W. Bush win the race.

Many Democrats condemned Ralph Nader for "taking" Gore's votes. His answer? "Throughout our history, these little parties got the ball rolling . . . What if voters had said, 'We're not going to vote for the anti-slavery party because they don't have a chance. We're going to vote for the least of the worst of the pro-slavery parties.'"

Nader points out an important role that third parties play in American politics. They have fought for important ideas such as ending slavery and using secret ballots for voting. If a third party's ideas get popular enough, the Democrats or Republicans often swoop them up. That usually takes away the third party's power, but at least its cause gets adopted into our political system.

Don't you wish the American Peace Party or the Free Pony and Ice Cream Political Party had been more powerful?

A WISH LIST OF NEW THIRD PARTIES
1. The Save All Endangered Species Party
2. The Wipe Out Cancer Party
3. The Watch More TV Party
4. The Birthday Party

Party Animals

The moose got into politics because of Teddy Roosevelt. Democrats and Republicans have animals as their symbols too. During Andrew Jackson's 1828 presidential campaign, his critics called him a jackass (another name for a donkey). Instead of being insulted, Democrat Jackson put a picture of this strong-minded animal on his campaign posters. Over time, the Democratic Party adopted the donkey as its symbol. Who could blame them? Until then, the animal linked to their party was the rooster.

Years later, a famous political cartoonist named Thomas Nast drew a picture of this Democratic donkey scaring a Republican elephant. The Republicans didn't like the cartoon. But they didn't mind being identified with such a dignified animal, so they used it to represent their party.

A lame duck doesn't seem dignified at all. Maybe that's why we've given this name to presidents who are finishing up their terms after a new president has been elected. The lame duck is on his way out, so he is seen to have less power.

Often the opposite is true. With nothing to lose, some

Thomas Nast's cartoon of 1874 linked the elephant with the Republican Party.

presidents make bold decisions. During his last days in office, Bill Clinton signed an order to protect millions of acres of federal forest from logging companies—a plan hated by incoming president George W. Bush.

Other members of the political zoo? A dark horse is a candidate nominated unexpectedly, one who comes from behind to win the race. Some people called Bill Clinton a dark horse. President Warren G. Harding certainly was. In 1920, Republicans couldn't decide between two other candidates and compromised on Harding, in large part because he looked like a president. But one senator knew better and offered some advice. "Don't let him make any speeches," he said.

ELECT ME. I'LL LOOK GREAT ON A STAMP?

Warren G. Harding

The people of Guffey, Colorado, weren't interested in horses of any kind. Instead, they elected a cat, Smudge le Plume, to be mayor of their town. Smudge was quite popular until she died mysteriously in 1991. Town officials investigated and ruled out political assassination. Smudge, they decided, had been eaten by an owl.

Then a golden retriever named Shanda became mayor. So now Guffey has two political parties: the Democats and the Repupkins.

Vote 4 le Plume

★ 2 ★
See How They Run

Throughout your life, you'll vote in many different elections. You'll pick the candidates you want to represent you in Washington DC. You'll vote for people to run your city or town. You may even vote for town dogcatcher or someone to oversee the local cemetery as they do in Warner, New Hampshire.

How do you learn enough about these people to decide if you like and trust them? It depends. Candidates run their campaigns differently. Dogcatchers don't make speeches on TV, promising to enforce pooper-scooper rules. Senators don't go door-to-door meeting everyone in their state.

At their best, campaigns alert us to what's important. They tell us what a candidate believes. They also make us think about where we stand. And, they help us understand why others hold a different point of view.

To get a picture of how the process works, here's a look at our most important election . . .

. . . one that is held every four years . . .

. . . the election of the president of the United States.

WARNING: Some of the history you are about to read may be hazardous to your health. The things that certain people have done to gain power are shocking, appalling, horrendous, dreadful, and dire. Democracy is a messy business. It's messy, in part, because we have freedom. Also, some people just don't play fair. Luckily others have worked hard to find and fix the problems.

My Name Is _____, and I Am Running for President!

You know how they say anyone can grow up to be president? Sorry, another myth bites the dust. (P.S. There's no such thing as a leprechaun, either.)

Arnold Schwarzenegger, who was born in Austria, could be the Terminator, the governor of California, even bodybuilding champion Mr. Universe—but never president of the United States. Our presidents must be born as American citizens.

Noah McCullough was born in Houston, Texas, and has already announced his plans to run. He has been on a ten-state tour. He has appeared on the *TODAY* show and *The Tonight Show*. He has even written two books, one about past presidents and another called *First Kids*. Noah is planning ahead. Presidents must be at least thirty-five years old, and Noah isn't quite there yet. He won't be old enough to run until 2032.

So far, our youngest elected president has been forty-three-year-old John F. Kennedy. The oldest, Ronald Reagan, was sixty-nine when he first became president. Four years later, people worried that he was too old to run again. Reagan made a joke of it. He said he wouldn't make age an issue in the campaign. He wouldn't criticize his fifty-six-year-old rival, Walter Mondale, for his "youth and inexperience."

Why do people run for office? Willam J. Bulow, who ran for governor of South Dakota in 1926, was ambitious, pure and simple. "There are no issues," he said. "My opponent has a job and I want it." Amazingly, he won!

Like Bulow, people running for president want power. Unlike Bulow, most want to serve their country. And they have ideas about how to make things better. Abraham Lincoln believed in keeping the North and South together and would fight the Civil War to do so. When a quarter of the nation was out of work during the Great Depression of the 1930s, Franklin Roosevelt wanted the government to create new jobs. In the 1970s, Richard Nixon and Jimmy Carter worked for peace by strengthening our relations with other countries.

A candidate's first task, however, is to convince his party that he is the right man to run. That she is the woman for the job.

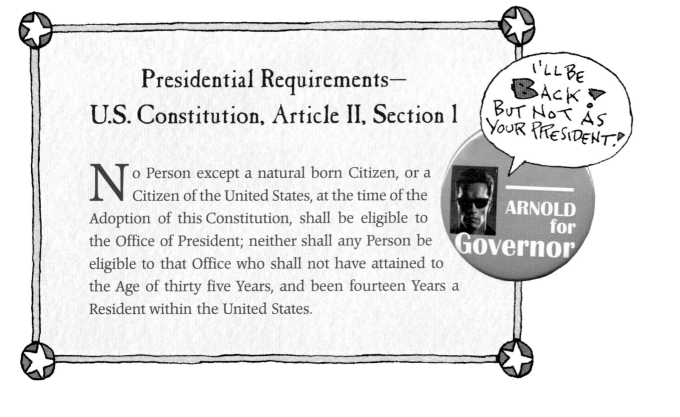

Presidential Requirements— U.S. Constitution, Article II, Section 1

No Person except a natural born Citizen, or a Citizen of the United States, at the time of the Adoption of this Constitution, shall be eligible to the Office of President; neither shall any Person be eligible to that Office who shall not have attained to the Age of thirty five Years, and been fourteen Years a Resident within the United States.

Primary Education

At the beginning of a presidential race, many politicians dream of winning the election. But each party will pick only one of them to run. How does each party decide which candidate best represents it? And has the best chance of winning?

Party leaders used to choose their candidates at national conventions (to learn about conventions, just turn the page). Today most states have some kind of primary, an election that lets ordinary party members vote for the person they want to run.

Seems strange, doesn't it? A primary is an election, but we don't get a president at the end of it. Each primary is a "pre-election election" that determines one state's choice for the candidate who will RUN for president.

Candidates use primaries to get party members and the media excited about them. Some of them also need to demonstrate that they are electable. They may have to prove they can overcome controversial parts of their past, such as divorce, or show that they have a chance to win this election after having lost others.

Kennedy for President?

Before 1960, no one thought a Catholic could win the presidency. So, John F. Kennedy had a lot to prove. When reporters announced that Kennedy was losing voters because of his religion, he attacked this prejudice. "I refuse to believe that I was denied the right to be president the day that I was baptized," he said.

Kennedy won the needed primaries, showing he had a chance to win the presidency. He got his party's nomination. And he became the first Catholic president of the United States.

Talk about candidates with something to overcome . . . what about Barack Obama and Hillary Clinton? They battled in the 2008 primaries to try to prove a dramatic first: an African American or a woman could win the Democratic nomination and then the election to become president.

Primary season starts in Iowa and New Hampshire. These two contests are so important that candidates start campaigning there years in advance.

Jimmy Carter did. When this former Georgia governor announced that he was running for president, few people outside the South knew him. In fact, reporters called him "Jimmy Who?" They also joked about his family's peanut farming business.

Carter started campaigning in New Hampshire two years before the 1976 election. He won its primary over five better-known Democratic candidates. Suddenly he was declared the favorite. That helped him win more primaries, then the nomination and the presidency.

All these primaries are mini-contests that decide who will compete in the mega contest—the November election for the president of the United States.

A Meeting of the Minds

In 1831, a political party called the Anti-Masons held the first national convention. Members from around the country gathered in a saloon in Baltimore, Maryland. They talked and argued and, by the end of the night, chose their candidate for president. They obviously had a good time doing it. The Democrats decided to meet in the same saloon the following year to pick theirs.

Since then, most political parties have had national conventions. Every four years, representatives of the party, called delegates, get together to select their presidential and vice presidential candidates. In the old days, party leaders controlled conventions by handpicking the delegates. After William McKinley and Teddy Roosevelt were nominated in 1900, one Republican leader told reporters, "I am glad that we had our way." Then he corrected himself quickly, "The people, I mean, had their way."

Conventions could be very rowdy events. At that 1900 convention, for example, two Texans, arguing over a seat, whacked each other until one drew a knife and onlookers broke up the quarrel. At another Republican convention, twelve years later, one candidate's supporters rubbed pieces of sandpaper together to drown out the speeches of any rivals.

The Democrats hold the record for the shortest convention (six hours in 1872) and the longest. In 1924, they simply could not decide upon a candidate. They voted and fought and voted 103 times until they settled on a candidate no one, including the American people, liked. The Democrats lost the presidency that year, but their seventeen-day meeting broke the record for the most hot dogs consumed and the most fistfights.

Score One for Democracy!

Party bosses used to pick the presidential nominee. But over the last forty years, ordinary people have fought for change. Now most delegates are chosen in elections by regular party members.

Agnew? Gesundheit!

In 1968, Richard Nixon wanted a running mate who wouldn't compete with him. He picked Spiro Agnew, the governor of Maryland. Nixon wanted someone unknown and got his wish. When a reporter went onto a busy city street to ask what Spiro Agnew was, one person said "a disease." Another suggested, "It's some kind of egg."

Today we have primary elections, and they have changed the way candidates are selected (if you don't know how, flip back to pages 30–31). Since 1976, every Democratic and Republican candidate has gone to his convention having already won the nomination in the primaries. Will the primary process mean the end of national conventions?

Probably not. There is no guarantee that a season of primaries will confirm which candidate will win the nomination. Then the delegates at the convention must make the decision. Furthermore, there are other important things that take place when a party gets together.

The nominee announces his choice of running mate, for example. This decision is an important one. Having a balanced team can attract more voters. A presidential candidate from the North might pick a Southern running mate. A conservative might pick someone with more liberal ideas.

Even when it's just a formality, the presidential and vice presidential candidates must be voted in by the delegates at the convention. The party also uses this time to create a platform, which explains its position on important issues such as education, defense, and health care.

Finally, the convention helps everyone get excited about the long race ahead. There are usually lots of balloons and music, speeches and singing. The nominee has been campaigning for a long time just to get this far. Now the real race has begun.

And it costs lots of money . . .

Who's Paying the Bills?

Getting elected costs money. George Washington learned this lesson at the beginning of his political career. He ran for the Virginia state legislature twice and lost twice. The third time was the charm. In 1758, he treated voters to 160 gallons of alcohol and got elected!

Campaigning is expensive. Traveling from speech to speech costs a lot, whether it's by horse and buggy or jet. And whether candidates and their staff stay in Ye Olde Inn or a Holiday Inn.

Campaign budgets went through the roof once candidates started advertising on television. In 1952, Republican Dwight Eisenhower was one of the first. He spent $6.6 million on his campaign, three times more than the last Republican candidate. In 2004, Democrat John Kerry and Republican George W. Bush spent a total of $620 million for TV time alone.

Most candidates don't have this kind of money in their own bank accounts. It has to come from somewhere else. Wouldn't it be great if people contributed money to campaigns just because they trusted a politician's opinions and goals? But sometimes people and organizations want something from a politician. They give him or her money and expect something in return.

When Republican Benjamin Harrison became president in 1888, he complained that he couldn't even pick his own staff. His campaign manager had already "sold out every place to pay the election expenses." In other words, people in industry had contributed to his campaign—and they were looking for payback.

This is one of those situations where democracy gets messy. Politicians need money to run their campaigns. Groups that represent everything from oil companies to good health care set aside money to contribute to politicians. Can candidates take money without being influenced by those who give it?

On one hand, some people think that supporting a candidate, even by giving lots of money, is an American right—the right of free speech.

On the other hand, some people want limits on campaign fund-raising. Being able to contribute huge sums gives an unfair advantage to the interests of rich people and organizations.

On another hand, people think that limits on raising money discourage good candidates from running.

On still another hand (whose hands are these, anyway?!), having to raise so much money keeps good candidates from running.

Over the last century, Congress has passed laws to limit the money that wealthy people and organizations can give. People have also found loopholes, legal ways to get around the rules. Recently, our Supreme Court decided that big companies can also contribute directly to candidates.

Some states aren't waiting for the federal government to figure it out. Since 2000, candidates running for state office in Maine and Arizona get public money for their campaigns if they don't take donations or use their own money. The cities of Portland, Oregon, and Albuquerque, New Mexico, passed similar laws in 2005. In 2010, Hawaii tried out their version of this system. City by city, state by state, the people are making changes.

What Would Ben Say?

Benjamin Franklin never ran for office, so he didn't have this problem. Once, however, he did say, "Pay what you owe and you'll know what's your own." He also said, however, "Nothing but money is sweeter than honey."

VOTE FOR ME AND A LITTLE LESS POLLUTION!

The Campaign Road

Long ago, politicians weren't supposed to seem as if they wanted to be president. So John Adams and Thomas Jefferson didn't dash around making speeches. It's just as well. Jefferson had a weak speaking voice. Adams had lost most of his teeth and spoke with a lisp.

This tradition went on for about a century. Ambitious men stayed home, pretending they were too noble to want the presidency. Meanwhile their fellow party members did all the hard work, campaigning for them.

In 1896, for example, Republican William McKinley said he wouldn't campaign. But if people wanted to come to him . . .

The nation loved the idea. Most days, reporters and thousands of admirers came to see McKinley at his home. He wouldn't give speeches, mind you, but he did manage to chat for a while on his front porch. Souvenir seekers shredded his picket fence to splinters. Don't feel bad for the McKinleys, though. They soon moved to a new house, a big white one in Washington DC.

Mark Hanna

The Man Behind the President—1896

Mark Hanna, a wealthy businessman, had been backing McKinley since he ran to become the governor of Ohio. In 1896, while McKinley was greeting visitors at home, Mark Hanna was getting him the presidency. He collected a fortune from other industrialists to launch the first all-out media campaign. Hanna hired one thousand four hundred people to make sure pictures of McKinley appeared everywhere. He also got cut-rate fares on railroads owned by his friends for the seven hundred fifty thousand people coming to visit McKinley!

P.S. Today's campaigns involve even more people.

Candidates finally got off their front porches and have been campaigning ever since. In 1948, Harry Truman traveled more than thirty thousand miles to meet the American people. In 1964, Lyndon Johnson covered sixty thousand miles in the final forty-two days.

William Jennings Bryan may not have traveled as far as more modern candidates, but this Democrat deserves the Determination Award. In 1908, Bryan made up to thirty speeches a day. He was so exhausted, his aides dumped cold water on him to wake him for his next appearance.

Being on the road is tiring for everyone. That's why George W. Bush brought his own pillow on the 2000 campaign trail. He always had a piece of home with him, no matter where he was sleeping.

Candidates work this hard to make sure the public knows who they are and what they stand for. They shake a gajillion hands and even kiss a few babies. They make speeches and give interviews to reporters for newspapers, radio, and TV. They debate other candidates to explain why their ideas are better than their opponents'.

Oh, Baby!

While campaigning in 1832, Andrew Jackson was handed a baby with a dirty, goopy face. "Here is a beautiful specimen of young American childhood," he exclaimed. Then he presented the baby to his friend. "Kiss him," Jackson demanded, and walked away.

Meanwhile the candidates' supporters are working too. In cities and towns all across the country, they are handing out information about the candidates and their views. They are making telephone calls and going door-to-door to spread the word.

Bumper stickers appear on cars with candidates' names and slogans. Campaign buttons have turned people into walking advertisements since our first elections. In fact, all sorts of campaign gimmicks have helped candidates become better known. Teddy Roosevelt had quite a smile; his supporters handed out Teddy's Teeth kazoos. Many John F. Kennedy fans wore vests proclaiming, "Kennedy is the Remedy."

The most popular campaign item ever was probably the whiskey handed out in log-cabin-shaped bottles made by the E.C. Booz Distillery for William Henry Harrison in 1840. It was a gift that lasted far longer than the whiskey. Harrison won and the word *booze,* meaning liquor, became part of our vocabulary.

A CANDIDATE'S WISH LIST

1. A Home Sweet Home sign to hang in each hotel room

2. More chocolates left on my pillow

3. No more kissing babies, yech-h-h!

4. Everybody votes for me!

Lights, Camera, Action!

In 1960, something new was happening. Presidential candidates were going to debate each other for the very first time. And on television!

On September 26, seventy million people turned on their sets. Democrat John F. Kennedy was wearing a dark suit. Republican Richard Nixon was wearing a gray one that blended in with the background. Kennedy was tan. Nixon, who had been sick, was tired and pale and refused to wear makeup. He looked as if he hadn't shaved.

They talked about many issues, including the economy and space exploration. Both expressed their ideas very well. When Nixon talked, he looked at Kennedy. Kennedy took a producer's advice. He looked at the camera so it seemed as if he were speaking directly to the American people.

Some people listened to this debate on the radio. The majority of them believed Nixon had won. But most people watching television thought Kennedy won. *He looked better.* The age of television campaigning had begun.

In the old, old days, people got information about elections from newspapers or from each other. Until photography was invented around the time of Abraham Lincoln, people had to rely on drawings to know what their presidents looked like.

As technology improved, Americans got closer to the news and their candidates. The telegraph sent election results across the country within minutes. By 1916, campaigns produced short political films to show in movie theaters. Starting in 1924, the nation could turn on radios to hear what was happening at national conventions.

For more than fifty years, television has brought politics into our living rooms. TV lets voters get to know their candidates. But it also means that a candidate's looks and personality are judged on camera. Who knows, would Teddy Roosevelt have seemed too hyper? How would John Adams have faired with his lisp and missing teeth?

Nixon wouldn't make the same mistakes today. Now candidates hire experts to improve their image. They get new haircuts, new outfits, trade eyeglasses for contacts.

In the olden days, people didn't see much of their candidates. Now we see them on TV talk shows. George W. Bush appeared on *The Oprah Winfrey Show.* Michelle and Barack Obama danced on *The Ellen DeGeneres Show.*

Is this better or worse? Are we getting to know our candidates as people or are they playing a part? Do we need to know our candidates as people? That's for us to decide. Democracy is a messy business, and it's our job to sort it out.

Recently it got even more complicated. Many people think the way Obama used the Internet during his first campaign had the same effect as Kennedy's TV debate. It was a political game changer. His videos were watched on YouTube for more than 14 million hours. His staff used the Internet to organize armies of supporters to work for their candidate. Reaching out to voters online prompted them to contribute money a little at a time (which can add up fast).

A Short History of
Political Buttons

What is the best way to learn about our candidates? The media can shape the way we think without our knowing it. A newspaper can choose not to run a story about a candidate if it's going to make him look bad. A TV station can give one story a lot of time and make it seem important. It can make another seem unimportant by barely mentioning it at all.

Sometimes the way a story is told makes a huge difference. Just look at these two headlines:

What does each one make you think and feel?

Debate on the Media

The Good News: With cable TV, we have many channels with different points of view.

The Bad News: Lots of people think that what they read in newspapers and see on TV is the truth, pure and simple. They forget that people in the media can choose the facts they want to use to express their opinions.

The Good News: The Internet is a great way to find even more information. We can read newspapers from different states or countries. We can debate—just like candidates—on blogs and social media.

The Bad News: Not all Web sites are created equal. You have to make sure a site has truthful, accurate information.

The Good News: You don't have to wait until you can vote to learn about politics in newspapers, on TV, and on the Web. And you don't have to wait to start expressing your opinions.

Sticks and Stones

The most important part of any campaign is telling people what a candidate stands for. As pressure grows, however, high-minded debates can turn to low-down name-calling. Campaign messages can boil down to: pick me because I'm wonderful and my opponent is a (fill in the blank yourself!).

Insults can be very creative. During the 1848 campaign, Whigs called Democratic candidate Lewis Cass a "pot-bellied, mutton-headed cucumber."

In 1916, the Democrats said that dignified-looking Republican Charles Evans Hughes was just an "animated feather duster." Even his fellow Republican Theodore Roosevelt called him "a bearded iceberg." Hughes was doomed.

Insults, however, can backfire. Democrat Stephen A. Douglas once called his Republican rival, Abraham Lincoln, "two-faced." Lincoln's reply? "If I had another face, do you think I would wear this one?"

Before running in 1960, John F. Kennedy wrote a book called *Profiles in Courage.* The Republicans liked to call him the "boy" with "too much profile and not enough courage."

Kennedy wasn't fazed at all. In a speech, he said that Nixon had called him lots of things, including "an economic ignoramus, a Pied Piper, and all the rest." He smiled at the audience and said, "I've just confined myself to calling him a Republican."

A CANDIDATE'S LIST
OF IMPUDENT INSULTS

He/She is a . . .
. . . blundering birdbrain.
. . . deplorable dolt.
. . . nattering nincompoop.
. . . sniveling sellout.

I STILL LIKE THIS ONE THE BEST!

Dirty Tricks

Every candidate expects an insult or two. But some politicians cross the line. They graduate to "dirty tricks"—underhanded ways to hurt an opponent.

Newspaperman James Callender accused President John Adams of planning to make himself king. He wrote that Adams, if reelected, would declare war on France. Candidate Thomas Jefferson, he said, would keep the peace.

What's wrong with that? Americans are allowed to express their views, aren't they? Yes, but Thomas Jefferson had paid Callender to write these opinions. This trick helped Jefferson to become our third president.

More than 150 years later, Republican Richard Nixon was vice president running for reelection. That year the Republican Convention was held in San Francisco. The city's garbage trucks passed the convention center on their way to the dump. Democrats put huge signs on the trucks that said, "Dump Nixon."

During his presidential campaign in 1972, Nixon pulled some dirty tricks of his own. Mountains of food were delivered to Democrats who never ordered it. Flyers advertised a free lunch given by Democrats that didn't really exist. Reservations for meeting halls were canceled right before rallies were supposed to begin.

Nixon's tricks got even dirtier. His campaign hired people to break into the headquarters of the Democratic National Committee at the Watergate Hotel. They were bugging the offices to listen to secret information. Discovery of this break-in led to Nixon's resignation in 1974. He is the only president who has ever resigned.

Oops! Bad Judgment Calls

Sometimes a rival's dirty tricks hurt a candidate's campaign. Other times, candidates create trouble for themselves.

In 1860, Democrat Stephen A. Douglas had a huge problem (besides Republican candidate Abraham Lincoln). Douglas's party was split over the issue of slavery, so many of its members wouldn't support him. Presidential candidates still weren't supposed to campaign, but Douglas was desperate. He came up with a story about going to "visit his mother." But his journey there twisted through cities and towns so he could give speeches all along the way.

When the Republicans found out, they started a campaign of their own. They posted signs wherever Douglas appeared. "A Boy Lost!" one exclaimed. Another, supposedly signed by Douglas's mother, asked if anyone had seen "her wandering son."

GOOD NEWS, MRS. DOUGLAS, I'VE FOUND YOUR SON!

Abraham Lincoln

Stephen A. Douglas

When Richard Nixon ran for president in 1960, candidates traveled everywhere. Almost everywhere. Nixon promised that he'd campaign in every state, including the new states of Alaska and Hawaii. The week before the election, Nixon still hadn't been to Alaska.

He had to make a choice. Should he fulfill his promise? Or should he spend the time campaigning in Texas and Illinois? Nixon went to Alaska and lost the two states that could have given him the election.

Sometimes one careless moment has a long, humiliating effect. In 1988, Democratic candidate Mike Dukakis wanted to look like a strong leader. So he had his picture taken riding in a tank. Dukakis was wearing a suit and tie—and a helmet that was much too big for him. He looked more like a goofy kid than a president. Unfortunately for him, the nation let him know it.

★ 3 ★
It's Showtime

By the time Election Day finally rolls around, everyone's ready to find out who the next president will be. Except, perhaps, the candidate who is losing!

Our Constitution doesn't give us too many rules about voting. It decrees only that anyone in the United States who is over eighteen is eligible to vote and can't be excluded because of race or gender. Lawmakers in each state decide the who, when, where, and how of voting within their borders. Over time these rules have changed, in large part to cut down on cheating.

Who? As long as a state obeys the Constitution, it can create its own rules about who can vote there. It determines, for example, how long someone must live in the state before voting. It decides if prisoners can vote, and nowadays only two states allow it.

States do let other people vote, even though they can't get to the polls. Sick or elderly citizens can mail in their votes on papers called absentee ballots. So can citizens who are traveling. And in Texas, where many astronauts live to be close to Johnson Space Center, residents can cast absentee ballots from space.

When? In olden times, Election Day was actually Election *Days*, nearly a week in some states. Finally each state agreed to use just one day for presidential elections, but then they picked different days! That worked well for dishonest party leaders, who herded men across state lines to vote twice. So, in 1845, a law set the presidential election on the first Tuesday after the first Monday in November. Why they didn't choose the second Wednesday after the first Tuesday is anybody's guess!

A LOSING CANDIDATE'S WISH LIST

1. More time
2. An enthusiastic endorsement from every living president
3. Better yet, endorsements from George Washington, Abraham Lincoln, and John F. Kennedy
4. More money
5. Winning the lottery so I can buy more TV ads
6. More time and money!!!

Where? New Englanders began by voting at their town meetinghouses, and some still do. Men (only men could vote then, remember?) in other states had to travel to the county courthouse, sometimes twenty miles away. That was no easy task in the days before automobiles.

States have gradually made voting districts smaller and smaller so people don't have as far to go. Now people vote in local schools, libraries, even the lobbies of apartment buildings. These polling places are run by trained workers, who make sure voters are registered and vote only once.

How? Voting methods have also changed. Up until the Civil War, Southern men went to the courthouse and simply announced whom they were voting for. By then, other places were putting votes on paper. In some locations, voters each brought their own sheet with names written on it. In others, each political party had its own distinctly colored ballot. So much for keeping your choices secret . . .

. . . until the Australian ballot was adopted by most states in the 1890s. Corrupt party leaders weren't too happy about this ballot, which listed the candidates from all the major parties and was handed out by government officials. Suddenly voting was more secret. It was also harder to cheat.

By the 1950s, half of Americans were voting by machine. They stepped behind a curtain for privacy. Then they voted by pulling levers next to their candidates' names.

The newest idea is replacing these machines with computerized ones. In some cases, voters punch holes in cards that are counted by computer. Or they mark choices on a ballot, then a computer scans their votes. Other times voters enter their choices directly onto the computer.

Is this progress? People aren't so sure. As you'll see, there were questions about how well these methods worked in the 2000 election.

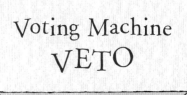

Voting Machine VETO

The first election using a voting machine took place in 1892. But Thomas Edison invented the first voting machine almost 25 years earlier. Edison wanted to sell his gizmo to Congress to speed up its votes.

One congressman's answer? "If there is any invention on earth that we don't want down here, that is it." The old-fashioned way of calling upon each representative for his vote gave them all more time to cut deals.

And the Winner Is . . .

As soon as the polls close, officials begin to count the votes. In the old days, it took a long time to sort and add the votes on paper ballots. Today, officials at some polling places still have to sort through paper ballots. They throw out spoiled ones—for example, ones that have two candidates marked for the same job. Then they count up the rest. Other polling places have computerized voting machines and get their tallies with just a few clicks. They report their results to state officials, and the count begins to rise.

In the olden days, it could take weeks for the news of a winner to travel through the country. At the beginning of the twentieth century, technology helped results come in faster. Some people gathered in auditoriums to hear the latest reports sent in by telegraph. Still others gathered outside newspaper offices to see the updated figures posted on bulletin boards or special screens. In some cities, searchlights shot different-colored beams into the sky to signal who was ahead.

Nowadays, TV, radio, and the Internet give us the results as they're coming in. Sometimes even before. Reporters ask people who they voted for when they're leaving the polls. By going to different cities and towns, they can often predict who will win a state long before all the votes are counted.

These predictions aren't always right. Early on Election Night in 2000, TV reporters said the state of Florida went to Democrat Al Gore. A while later, they said it was too close to call. In the middle of the night, they reported that George W. Bush won the state, which, by then, meant he won the entire election. Al Gore called Bush to concede and was about to make a public announcement, when reporters said, once more, it was just too close to call.

WHAT WAS GOING ON? Good question, and as you'll see later, it's one that experts are still wondering about.

AND THE WINNER IS...

Gore's Final Bow

When Al Gore finally conceded the election, he announced, "Just moments ago, I spoke with George W. Bush and congratulated him on becoming the forty-third president of the United States, and I promised him that I wouldn't call him back this time."

Oops!

This is one of the most famous pictures in American history—a very happy Truman holding a newspaper with a very wrong headline. Dewey was leading the race when the *Chicago Daily Tribune* had to go to press. The reporters' best guess wasn't so good after all.

In 2000, it took only a few hours for reporters to realize they were wrong. The election of 1948 was another story. Two-thirds of the newspapers backed Republican candidate Thomas Dewey over Democratic president Harry Truman throughout the campaign. Before the election, fifty political experts predicted a landslide victory for Dewey.

Truman's answer? "Not one of them has enough sense to pound sand in a rathole."

It turns out Truman was right. On November 2, he won 303 electoral votes to Dewey's 189. When he returned to Washington DC, a huge sign was hanging on the building where the *Washington Post* newspaper was printed. It said, "Mr. President, we are ready to eat crow whenever you are ready to serve it."

Dewey sent Truman a telegram congratulating him on his victory. Nowadays, television makes winning and losing very public. The losing presidential candidate makes a speech in front of the cameras. He thanks all the people who helped with his campaign. Then he says that it's time for them to forget their differences and for the country to work together. He is always gracious. Who knows what he is really thinking?

One for You, Two for Me!

Yup, stealing is wrong. That hasn't stopped politicians from stealing votes here and there. Sometimes whole elections.

Their schemes have ranged from mild to outrageous. Candidates used to give out food and alcohol on Election Day, for example, hoping the way to a man's vote was through his stomach. Other times, they served up a "knuckle sandwich" instead. During the election of 1840, the Whigs and the Democrats hired gangsters to beat up rival party members to keep them from voting.

The Whigs and Democrats were still at it four years later. In New York City, for example, their presidential candidates for 1844, James K. Polk and Henry Clay, received fifty-five thousand votes between them. That's pretty impressive, considering only forty-five thousand New Yorkers were registered to vote!

Party officials in New York weren't the only ones to add fake voters. One politician padded Philadelphia's voting lists with fictional characters and household pets. Even George Washington and Benjamin Franklin were registered. As he said, "These fathers of American liberty voted down here once. And they vote here yet."

What Would Ben Say?

Ben once said, "[I'm] sorry I was born so soon, since I cannot have the happiness of knowing what will be known a hundred years hence." But if he knew about these election antics, he'd say, "Oh, my bejeebers!"

Notorious Democratic
Party Leader Boss Tweed

That trick was pretty outrageous. But no one could beat Boss Tweed, the Democratic leader of New York City politics in the middle of the nineteenth century. He kept the barbers busy on Election Day. First his men voted with full beards. Next they returned with mustaches or long sideburns. Finally they cast their ballots clean shaven. Using different hats, coats, and names each time, they managed to get past poll officials.

Tweed's motto? "Vote early and often."

Many New Yorkers voted for the Democrats and got favors in return. Before one election, Tweed's judge granted citizenship to Irish immigrants. In just twenty days, he swore in sixty thousand new citizens—in other words, sixty thousand new Democrat voters!

If these tricks weren't enough, Tweed's gang used other sneaky tricks as well. Voters in Republican districts were led to polling places with shorter lines. They were fake, so the votes were never counted. In other districts, Tweed's men put pencil lead under their thumbnails. When it was time to tally votes, they would mark up and spoil ballots cast for unwanted candidates.

Meanwhile in the South, former slaves had troubles of their own. In some places, federal troops made sure African American men could vote. In others, gangs of white men threatened the new voters or changed polling locations at the last minute.

Unfortunately election theft isn't just ancient history. In the 1940s, poor Mexican Americans in Texas were often paid for their votes. If they couldn't read, their ballots were already marked for them. Or, they were given strings with knots. When the string was placed alongside the ballot, it lined up with the names of the right candidates.

In Baltimore, Maryland, voting machines "magically" broke down during the hours when Republicans usually voted. They would be "fixed" in time for Democrats voting later in the day. In other cities, medicine was slipped into the coffee of election officials, timed so they would be sick in the bathroom—allowing others to "count" the votes for them.

Then there was the man in New York City who was very enthusiastic about a Republican primary election in the 1970s. He was arrested, but not before he voted sixty-eight times!

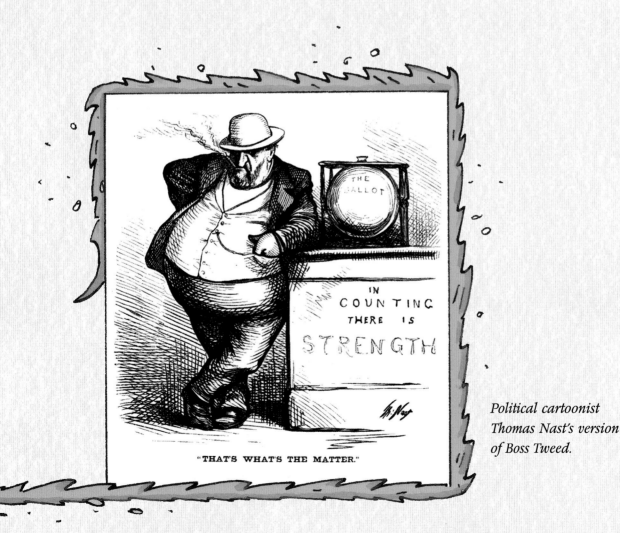

Political cartoonist Thomas Nast's version of Boss Tweed.

★ 4 ★
Hail to the New Chief

New presidents don't take office right away. In the early days, it took a long time for officials to collect election results and for winners to travel to Washington. Inaugurations, the ceremony when one president replaces another, didn't take place until March 4. Eventually Congress decided that trains, planes, and telephones made this long a wait unnecessary. Now inaugurations are held on January 20.

At noon, every new president takes the same oath that George Washington did—more or less. Washington solemnly swore to do his job. Swearing was against Franklin Pierce's religion; he "affirmed" instead.

Typically new presidents are sworn (or affirmed) into office on the steps of the Capitol by the head of the Supreme Court. Typically the old president is there too. Outgoing president John Quincy Adams was so angry he lost to Andrew Jackson that he refused to show up.

Historic Inaugural Firsts

April 30, 1789. George Washington. His inauguration simply was the first.

Mom

March 4, 1881. James Garfield. Garfield was the first to have his mother come with him to the ceremony.

March 4, 1921. Warren G. Harding. Harding was the first president to ride to and from his inauguration in an automobile.

The first act a new president does is make a speech. Washington's was the shortest one—135 words. William Henry Harrison's was the longest, at 8,445 words. Despite a heavy snowstorm, Harrison spoke for two hours without wearing a coat, hat, or gloves. As a result, he wasn't our ninth president for long. He caught a cold and died of pneumonia one month later.

Many important people attend these inaugurations. Keeping them safe can be complicated. George W. Bush's second inauguration was held after the terrorist attacks on September 11. More than one hundred square blocks were closed off. Fighter jets patrolled the skies; thirteen thousand police officers and soldiers guarded the streets. Security was even tighter in 2008 for the inauguration of our first African American president, Barack Obama.

President Lincoln had sharpshooters protecting him while he was sworn in. Actually, he needed them earlier. Al Pinkerton, a

famous detective, uncovered a plot to assassinate Lincoln in the Baltimore train station on his way to Washington. He convinced the president-elect to cancel a dinner in Philadelphia and board the train early. They sped through Baltimore hours ahead of schedule and made it to Washington safely.

Nowadays, presidents have lots of parties to celebrate their inaugurations. Bill Clinton had fourteen balls and danced at every one. But no one had a party quite like Andrew Jackson.

Jackson, our seventh president, was from the Wild West. Many of his frontier buddies came to his party at the White House. His guests got so rowdy—breaking dishes, tearing down curtains, standing on furniture—that Jackson snuck out and spent the night at a hotel. Finally servants dragged tubs of punch onto the lawn. It was the only way they could get the crowd out of the White House.

"... BEFORE CONCLUDING, FELLOW-CITIZENS, I MUST SAY SOMETHING TO YOU ON THE SUBJECT OF THE PARTIES AT THIS TIME EXISTING IN OUR COUNTRY. TO ME IT APPEARS... COUGH... PERFECTLY CLEAR THAT THE INTEREST OF THAT COUNTRY REQUIRES THAT THE VIOLENCE OF THE SPIRIT BY WHICH THOSE PARTIES ARE... COUGH, COUGH... AT THIS TIME... COUGH... GOVERNED MUST BE GREATLY MITIGATED, IF NOT ENTIRELY EXTINGUISHED, OR CONSEQUENCES WILL ENSUE WHICH ARE APPALLING TO BE THOUGHT OF. IF PARTIES... COUGH, COUGH... IN A...."

August 3, 1923. Calvin Coolidge. After Harding died, Coolidge was the first president to be sworn into office by his own father, who was a notary public in Vermont.

March 4, 1933.
January 20, 1937.
January 20, 1941.
January 20, 1945.
Franklin Delano Roosevelt. Roosevelt was the first—and last—president inaugurated for a third or fourth term. The Twenty-second Amendment, ratified in 1951, limits presidents to two terms.

The Other Route to the White House

For a long time, the vice presidency was not seen as much of a prize. When asked to be vice president, Daniel Webster said, "I do not intend to be buried until I am dead." The thirty-second vice president, John Nance Garner, supposedly proclaimed that the job was "not worth a pitcher of warm spit."

But one second can change everything. When a president dies in office, the vice president becomes very, very important. This is how eight of our VPs have become commander in chief.

Ironically, the Republican Party put Teddy Roosevelt in this job to get him out of the way. In fact, one leader told President McKinley, "Your duty to the country is to live for four years."

McKinley didn't do his duty. He was assassinated less than six months later. Roosevelt became president and had the next three years to win over the American people. His critics called him "His Accidency," but he won the next election and was president for another four years.

Vice President Calvin Coolidge didn't do a lot of talking. He seemed like such a sourpuss that someone said he'd been "weaned on a pickle." Once a dinner guest told him that she'd bet she could make him say more than two words to her. His answer? "You lose!"

Calvin Coolidge

This is not the kind of guy who wins elections. Luckily he didn't have to. When Warren G. Harding died of a heart attack in 1923, "Silent Cal" became the thirtieth president of the United States. Believe it or not, he won the 1924 election too. The American public liked his calm nature. So when a man came up to him and said, "I didn't vote for you," Coolidge could quickly reply, "Someone did."

The Presidential Lineup

Gerald Ford was the ninth VP to be promoted midterm. He was the only vice president to become president without being elected to either position. Ford had been House Minority Leader and became vice president when Spiro Agnew resigned in disgrace in 1973. He became president ten months later, when Richard Nixon resigned as well.

After vice president and Speaker of the House of Representatives, the order of succession is:

President pro tempore of the Senate
Secretary of State
Secretary of the Treasury
Secretary of Defense
Attorney General
Secretary of the Interior
Secretary of Agriculture
Secretary of Commerce
Secretary of Labor
Secretary of Health and Human Services
Secretary of Housing and Urban Development
Secretary of Transportation
Secretary of Energy
Secretary of Education
Secretary of Veterans Affairs
Secretary of Homeland Security

★ 5 ★
Uncle Sam Wants You

When your generation becomes old enough to vote, you will have a huge voice—more than seventy-three million strong. Imagine what seventy-three million votes can do . . .

✓ Improve schools

✓ Make sure no kid goes hungry

✓ Work toward world peace—of course!

You are going to have a chance to change things. In fact, you can start right now. And that's a good thing, because our democracy needs you . . .

A KID'S WISH LIST
of Future Political Goals

1. Send astronauts to Mars
2. Send Mars bars to Mars
3. Declare ice cream a vegetable
4. World peace—of course!

Here's What You're Up Against!

For most of our history, voting was a really big deal. Before we had absentee ballots, traveling salesmen, government workers in Washington DC, even soldiers returned to their home states to vote. People waited in line patiently for hours. They took off work and celebrated with picnics and parades, just like on the Fourth of July.

Voting and citizenship went hand in hand.

Starting in the mid-1960s, our country went through a time of great upheaval. Struggles around civil rights and the Vietnam War split the nation. Watergate (see "Dirty Tricks," page 47) tested people's faith in our leadership.

Many Americans began to feel as if politicians didn't care about them. The change in campaign methods didn't help either. Television took our candidates out of meeting halls and put them onto a little screen. People lost a feeling of connection with their leaders and the political process. They stopped trusting the system.

By the 1970s, more people could vote than ever before. The law had changed so citizens over eighteen years old could vote. Minorities who had once been discriminated against could get to the polls. Registering—signing up to vote—got even easier. Yet fewer people were registering, let alone showing up on Election Day. The number of possible voters who actually cast a ballot dropped from an all-time high of 83 percent to about 50 percent.

And the younger Americans who could now vote? Only 50 percent took part in their first possible election in 1972. By 1998, that figure dropped to a sorry 20 percent.

A democracy isn't a democracy if its people don't take part.

Five Bucks on the Dark Horse in November

Another reason why elections used to be more exciting? Before polls predicted outcomes, people rarely knew who was going to win. They stayed hopeful about their candidate till the end and felt as if their vote mattered. They also gambled on the outcome. A lot. Even the *New York Times* would report the changing odds. Gambling on elections dwindled in the 1940s. Perhaps that was because it finally became legal to bet on horse races.

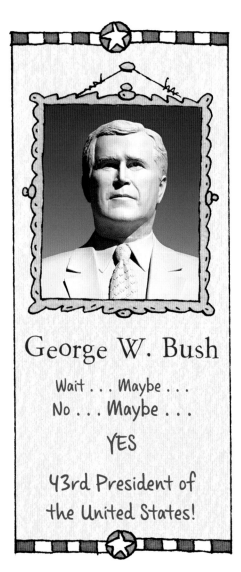

George W. Bush

Wait ... Maybe ...
No ... Maybe ...

YES

43rd President of
the United States!

Knock, Knock.
Who's There?
President.
President Who?

What good is a democracy if its people don't take part?

And what if they do take part and feel as if their voices are not heard? In 2000, for the first time since 1888, a candidate won the popular vote and lost the presidency. Yup, that old electoral college issue again.

The electoral college was just part of the controversial contest between Democrat Al Gore and Republican George W. Bush. Let's recap what you've read about this race so far. The election was very close . . . whoever won in Florida would win the presidency . . . TV reporters said Gore won Florida . . . then took it back . . . they said Bush won . . . then took it back.

By the morning after Election Day, Bush had won Florida by so few votes that state law said they must be recounted. Democrats and Republicans fought about how this should be done. Florida state judges made some decisions about the process. But the fight went all the way to the U.S. Supreme Court, which finally voted 5–4 to stop the recount. On December 13, thirty-six days after the election, Bush claimed victory.

The final "official" tally in Florida had Bush ahead by 537 votes out of more than 6 million cast. Many people thought the election was unfair. Too many mistakes made the count untrustworthy. Ballots, printed in a confusing way, led voters to pick a third-party candidate whose name was across from Gore's. Old voting machines lost almost 3 percent of the votes.

Both parties threw accusations at each other. Words like *fraud* and *theft* and *dirty tricks* were used.

Among other things, the Democrats claimed:
- Roadblocks set up on Election Day made it harder for voters to get to their polling places. Most of these roadblocks were in Democratic parts of the state.
- In primarily white counties, voting machines let voters know if they mismarked their ballots and gave them a chance to fix any mistakes. In predominantly African American districts, where people usually vote for Democrats, the machines weren't set up the same way. If these voters made mistakes, their ballots were rejected and not counted.
- The members of the U.S. Supreme Court who voted to stop the recount were all appointed by a Republican president.

Among other things, the Republicans claimed:
- When TV reporters first announced that Gore won Florida, some of the state's western polling places were still open. This section of Florida is heavily Republican. People there might not have voted because they heard that Bush had already lost.
- Democrats cheated during the recount process, sneaking Bush ballots into Gore piles.
- The judges on the Florida Supreme Court were appointed by Democrats. They made decisions favoring their own party and not the law.

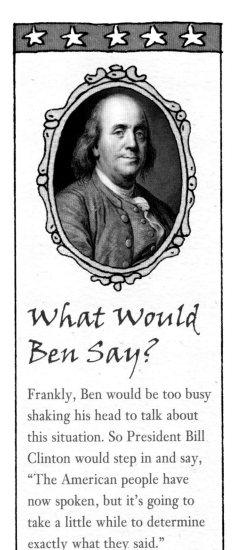

What Would Ben Say?

Frankly, Ben would be too busy shaking his head to talk about this situation. So President Bill Clinton would step in and say, "The American people have now spoken, but it's going to take a little while to determine exactly what they said."

Who lost? Al Gore, certainly. The American people did too; the way this election was handled disturbed them. One study shows that more than a third of the American people don't trust these election results. Almost half think something like this could happen again.

Crises help us make changes. The 2000 election got people thinking about election reform. The Help America Vote Act was passed in 2002 so states could upgrade their voting machines. Many people, including President Jimmy Carter, think that isn't enough. We need to keep working to ensure fair, honest elections.

Bad Chads

Election 2000 taught Americans about chads, the tiny bits of paper created when voters mark their choice by punching through a paper ballot. People debated about how to count ballots when chads didn't detach completely. What about hanging chads (still attached to the ballot by one corner), swinging chads (attached by two), and pregnant chads (completely attached, but bulging from a voter's efforts)? The clearest result of this discussion was that "Chad" dropped from the 239th most popular name for boys to the 338th—right below Marvin.

On the Rebound

Just when it looked like it couldn't get worse . . . it didn't!

Voter turnout in 2004 was the highest since 1968. In 2008, it jumped even higher. Best of all, the youth vote (defined, believe it or not, as voters aged eighteen to twenty-nine) was responsible for at least 60 percent of this increase. Young people can be a force in American politics if they want to be. If they show up.

We're making progress in the voting department, but most other democracies are still beating us. The United States is ranked 139th out of 172 countries in voter participation. Ouch! In other words, the first modern democracy (that's us) is near the bottom of the let's-get-out-the-vote list.

What would Benjamin Franklin say? Perhaps it's best just to imagine his comment this time!

The World's Best Voters*

1. Italy
2. Seychelles
3. Cambodia
4. Iceland
5. Angola
6. Indonesia
7. Somalia
8. New Zealand
9. Uzbekistan
10. South Africa
.
.
.
139. The United States of America

*Turnout measured in all elections since 1945

Borrowing ideas from other democracies was good enough for Ben and George. How are some of the 138 countries ahead of us getting their people to vote?

Australia's turnout is a whopping 95 percent. Their law says that citizens must vote. Actually, Australian law says citizens must go to the polls. Once they're there, you'd think they'd do their democratic duty. But they could write in Katie the Koala for senator if they wanted.

France and Japan vote on Sunday, Australia on Saturday. Weekend voting helps working people get to the polls. American law says we must vote on the first Tuesday after the first Monday in November. Should we change this law to vote on the first Saturday after the second Sunday? The third Sunday after the first Tuesday? Should we simply make Election Day a work-free holiday?

Sweden allows noncitizens who live legally in its country to vote. (Most of our states gave noncitizens the same right until the early 1900s!)

Germany and Denmark are among the countries that allow inmates to vote. Most democracies give people released from prison the same rights as other citizens. In the United States, about 5.3 million Americans—in or already out of prison—can't vote because they have been convicted of a crime.

Switzerland is testing out voting on the Internet. England is letting voters mail in their ballots. The state of Oregon has tried that too. As a result, 87 percent of Oregon voters participated in the 2004 presidential election.

Iowa and New Hampshire aren't foreign countries. But they are two of seven states that let people register when they come to vote instead of making them do it beforehand. Five of these states have the highest voter turnout in the nation.

Voter turnout in Costa Rica is typically about 90 percent. People think it's because Costa Rican kids accompany their parents to the polls. That's one practice we could start right now!

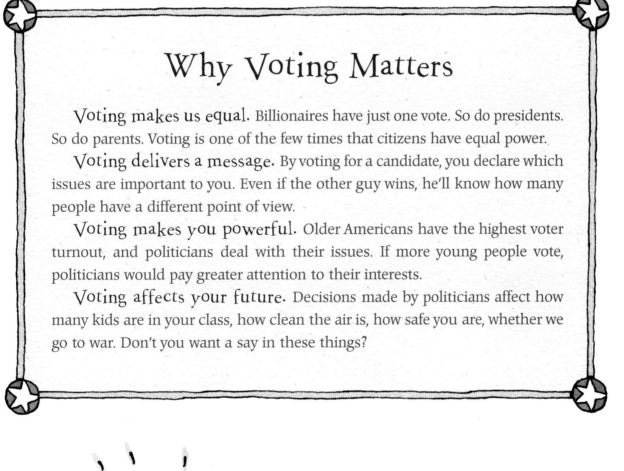

Why Voting Matters

Voting makes us equal. Billionaires have just one vote. So do presidents. So do parents. Voting is one of the few times that citizens have equal power.

Voting delivers a message. By voting for a candidate, you declare which issues are important to you. Even if the other guy wins, he'll know how many people have a different point of view.

Voting makes you powerful. Older Americans have the highest voter turnout, and politicians deal with their issues. If more young people vote, politicians would pay greater attention to their interests.

Voting affects your future. Decisions made by politicians affect how many kids are in your class, how clean the air is, how safe you are, whether we go to war. Don't you want a say in these things?

Just One Vote

If it's storming on Election Day, even committed voters may be tempted to stay home. If they have a cough or if a favorite program is on TV, some will ask themselves: does one vote really matter?

• In 1839, Marcus Morton was elected governor of Massachusetts by getting one more vote than his opponent. His new nickname, "Landslide," was sort of a joke, but he probably didn't care.

• Herbert Connolly lost track of time while campaigning for a seat on the Massachusetts Governor's Council in 1988. When he went to vote, the polls had just closed. He lost his own election by one vote.

• In Sydney Nixon's case, "just one vote" mattered twice! In 1997, he won his election for Vermont state representative by one vote—570 to 569. Then there was a recount and he lost—572 to 571.

Other important decisions have been decided by one vote as well.

• In 1868, the U.S. Senate voted on removing President Andrew Johnson from office. He won the right to stay—by one vote.

• Amendments to the Constitution must be approved by three-quarters of the states. In 1920, one more state was needed to approve the amendment giving women the right to vote. The Tennessee state legislature was tied. Twenty-two-year-old Harry Burns had planned to vote against it. He changed his mind and broke the tie. His mother asked him to.

• In 1997, a tie vote defeated a bill allowing Massachusetts to execute prisoners. The tie occurred because one state representative, who had voted for the death penalty earlier, changed his vote.

Rx for Voting

When people are involved with their communities, their knowledge of politics grows. Their interest and commitment does too. That's true for kids as well as grown-ups.

Okay, you aren't old enough to vote, not even close. But you can still have a voice in our democracy.

More than four millions kids already cast ballots on Election Day. They're part of a program called Kids Voting USA in schools in nineteen states and Washington DC. True, their votes aren't counted in official tallies. But they're announced in schools and on local TV stations.

This program has another advantage. Kids get so excited that 3 to 5 percent more of their parents end up voting too.

That's where you come in, even if Kids Voting USA isn't in your school. You can make sure your parents are registered to vote. And you can make sure they actually do it.

How? Oh, come on. How do you get your parents to do anything? Drive you somewhere? Buy a new game? Let you stay up late?

You bug 'em!

So bug them about voting. Plaster a countdown calendar on the front door. Put reminders on their voice mail. E-mail too. If they say they're too tired on the Big Day, try a bribe (it works when they want something from you!). Offer to do the dishes if they go—but only if you're desperate!

Pest Patrol

Who else can you pester into the polls?

- Grandparents
- Aunts and uncles
- Teachers
- Coaches
- Neighbors
- Dentist
- Cashier at the supermarket

Kids to the Rescue!

Bugging your parents is a good first step. Some kids are going even further. They are identifying issues and working on them. A recent report found that 55 percent of American kids volunteer. That's almost twice as many as adults.

Kids are becoming leaders . . .

Talk about bugging, a group of second graders decided that Massachusetts needed an official state insect. When they learned that any state resident could give legislators ideas for new laws, they got busy. Maybe it was the ladybug costumes they wore while visiting the state capitol. Maybe it was their speech saying ladybugs could be found all over the state. Whatever the reason, the legislature approved their bill and the governor signed a law proclaiming the ladybug as Massachusetts's state insect.

Third and fourth graders did something similar for New Hampshire, which didn't have a state fruit. The hardest thing about that process was convincing legislators that the pumpkin IS a fruit.

At age seven, Shadia Wood learned that the Superfund bill would clean up New York's worst toxic waste sites. For seven years, Shadia and a group called Kids Against Pollution tried to convince lawmakers to pass this bill. She had a lemonade stand on the steps of the state capitol, selling drinks and "toxic dump" cake. Then she'd send the profits to the governor to help pay for the Superfund. Eventually TV and newspaper reporters noticed what she was doing. The Superfund bill became law in 2003. (There's nothing wrong with shaming grown-ups into good behavior.)

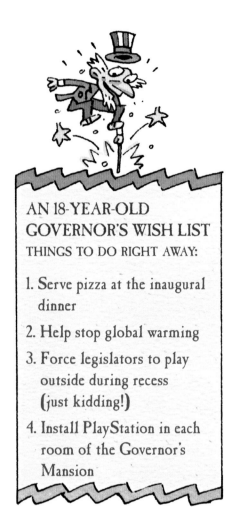

AN 18-YEAR-OLD
GOVERNOR'S WISH LIST
THINGS TO DO RIGHT AWAY:

1. Serve pizza at the inaugural dinner

2. Help stop global warming

3. Force legislators to play outside during recess (just kidding!)

4. Install PlayStation in each room of the Governor's Mansion

Imagine getting $135 to skip school and do good work? When Massachusetts's governor signed a bill to let sixteen- and seventeen-year-olds work at the polls, Boston-based students began helping voters with computerized equipment on Election Day. It's a win-win-win-win situation: kids know computers better than many adult voters; they get involved with voting; they get money. They are also being trained for the job. Our country will need them soon. The average poll worker is currently seventy-two years old.

In Boise, Idaho, kids ages fifteen and up are on committees governing the city. Some towns, like Linesville, Pennsylvania, have had eighteen-year-old mayors. Mayor at eighteen seems pretty great. But in California, Ohio, Rhode Island, Vermont, Washington, and Wisconsin, an eighteen-year-old can be governor.

Sending a Message

If you see a problem in your community or have an idea of how to make things better, get active. Give a government leader a piece of your mind (the best part, please!).

- Speak up at a town meeting.
- Invite your mayor or another official to speak to your class about an important issue. Be ready to ask good questions and give your opinions.
- Set up a class trip to visit him or her.
- Write a letter or e-mail that identifies a problem. Tell how the problem affects you and your community. Write about the changes you'd like to see. Send your letter to the appropriate official in your town or to your state representative and senator or to your representative and senator in Congress or even to the governor or president.
- Write a letter and get people who agree with you to sign it too. Make sure you write your names and addresses clearly.
- Make a survey about the problem, write it up, and send it to the right official.
- Be political online! Express your views on blogs, YouTube, Twitter, Facebook, or wherever kids are talking.

Or, as Ben Says . . .

"If you would not be forgotten, as soon as you are dead and rotten, either write things worth reading or do things worth the writing."

A Preachy but True Ending

Sometimes it seems as if things never, ever change. But they do.

In the United States of 1800, women couldn't be doctors or lawyers or even go to college. They could in 1900, but they still couldn't vote. At the beginning of the twenty-first century, Democrat Hillary Clinton made two serious runs to be the first woman president.

In the United States of 1800, most African Americans were slaves. In 1900 most African American men had the right to vote, but they were still enslaved by the prejudice that blocked them from the polls. At the beginning of the twenty-first century, Democrat Barack Obama became the first African American president.

In the United States of 1800, the Bill of Rights had already guaranteed religious freedom. Yet every president was Protestant for another 160 years until Catholic John F. Kennedy was elected in 1960. At the beginning of the twenty-first century,

Jewish Democrat Joseph Lieberman ran for vice president. In 2012 Republican Mitt Romney was making a serious run to be the first president who belonged to the Church of Jesus Christ of Latter-day Saints (also known as the Mormon religion).

When the first female African American president (with a Mormon father and a Jewish mother!) gets sworn into office, she will make history. But American voters should take most of the credit. They will have put her there.

Most important changes in our democracy start with the people, not politicians. Individuals, then small groups, and finally huge numbers of Americans opposed slavery. Workers went on strike to get better conditions on the job. Women demonstrated for the vote. African Americans marched for their rights. People fought for change and voted for leaders who would do the same. Then these politicians passed the laws and amendments that turned these struggles into achievements.

Democracy is a conversation between the people and their leaders, with newspapers, TV, and the Internet helping to spread the word. Sometimes it's a chat, sometimes a spat, and sometimes a SCREAMING MATCH. All are okay—as long as we don't stop talking.

Of course, listening isn't such a bad idea either!

Ben's Final Words

"Tell me and I forget.
Teach me and I remember.
Involve me and I learn."

Presidential Facts
Want to get to know our presidents better?

George Washington
1789 to 1797

Washington believed that shaking hands was beneath a president's dignity, so he bowed to his visitors instead.

John Adams
1797 to 1801

Adams was the first president to live in the White House. When he moved in, the residence didn't include a bathroom, only an outhouse in the backyard.

Thomas Jefferson
1801 to 1809

Jefferson wrote his own epitaph, listing many of his accomplishments but not his being president.

James Madison
1809 to 1817

Madison thought his voice was too annoying for him to be able to become a minister, so he went into politics instead.

James Monroe
1817 to 1825

In 1821 Monroe received every electoral vote except one. That delegate didn't want to spoil George Washington's record as the only president elected unanimously.

John Quincy Adams
1825 to 1829

Adams owned a pet alligator, which he kept in the East Room of the White House.

Andrew Jackson
1829 to 1837

For years Jackson carried two bullets in his body: one in his shoulder and one in his left lung. Both were lodged there as the result of duels.

Martin Van Buren
1837 to 1841

Van Buren was the first president born in the United States, but he grew up speaking a foreign language because his parents were Dutch.

William Henry Harrison
1841

Harrison had thought about becoming a doctor. It would have helped him when he developed pneumonia after his outdoor inauguration speech.

John Tyler
1841 to 1845

President Tyler was a busy man. He had fifteen children, eight with his first wife and (after she died) seven with his second.

James K. Polk
1845 to 1849

President Polk established a tradition by hosting the first annual Thanksgiving dinner at the White House.

Zachary Taylor
1849 to 1850

Taylor always refused to pay the extra postage if someone sent him a letter without enough stamps. That's why he didn't learn about his nomination for president until almost a week after it happened.

Millard Fillmore
1850 to 1853

Fillmore is the only president with two double l's in his name.

Franklin Pierce
1853 to 1857

During his second year in college, Pierce had the lowest grades in his class. He changed his study habits and graduated third in his class, even though his classmates included Nathaniel Hawthorne and Henry Wadsworth Longfellow.

James Buchanan
1857 to 1861

People sometimes thought Buchanan was strange because he would close one eye and leave the other open. Actually, he was farsighted in one eye and nearsighted in the other, so he did this to be able to see well.

Abraham Lincoln
1861 to 1865

Lincoln was the first president to die by assassination. He was shot in Washington DC, watching the same play that was being performed in Chicago on the day he was nominated for president—in Chicago.

Andrew Johnson
1865 to 1869

Andrew Johnson was illiterate when he got married at age eighteen. His wife taught him how to read and write.

Ulysses S. Grant
1869 to 1877

This president was born Hiram Ulysses Grant, but a West Point clerk enrolled him as Ulysses Simpson Grant by mistake. Grant kept that new name. He was embarrassed to be a soldier with initials that spelled out "HUG."

Rutherford B. Hayes
1877 to 1881

Hayes was the first president to have a telephone in the White House. It was installed by the inventor himself, Alexander Graham Bell.

James Garfield
1881

Garfield was assassinated, but it wasn't the bullet that killed him. Doctors tried to dig it out with dirty fingers and tools. Garfield died of blood poisoning.

Chester A. Arthur
1881 to 1885

Arthur loved to stay up late at night—and to sleep late, too. He often ate breakfast when he should have been eating lunch.

Grover Cleveland
1885 to 1889
1893 to 1897

This minister's son was the only president who hanged a man. While he was sheriff of Erie County, New York, he was also its executioner.

Benjamin Harrison
1889 to 1893

Harrison was the grandson of William Henry Harrison, who died after the cold he caught during his inauguration grew into pneumonia. Benjamin took no chances; he wore a full set of long underwear to his inauguration.

William McKinley
1897 to 1901

Except for George Washington, presidents shake a lot of hands. To keep from getting too sore, McKinley would squeeze a man's hand warmly before his own got caught in a hard grip.

Theodore Roosevelt
1901 to 1909

Roosevelt's eyesight was so bad that he could not recognize his own sons without his glasses.

William H. Taft
1909 to 1913

Taft owned the last cow that lived at the White House. A household pet, Pauline grazed on the lawn and provided milk for the family.

Woodrow Wilson
1913 to 1921

Wilson didn't learn the alphabet until nine years old and could not read until twelve. But he became president of Princeton University and president of the United States.

Warren G. Harding
1921 to 1923

Warren wasn't the only member of the Harding family who worked in Washington DC. His sister was a local policewoman.

Calvin Coolidge
1923 to 1929

Calvin Coolidge shared his presidential home with countless dogs, cats, and birds, two raccoons, a donkey, a bobcat named Smokey, lion cubs, a wallaby, a bear, and a pygmy hippo.

Herbert Hoover
1929 to 1933

President Hoover and his wife spoke in Chinese when they didn't want to be understood. Wealthy by the time he got to the White House, Hoover donated his entire presidential salary to charity.

Franklin D. Roosevelt
1933 to 1945

Roosevelt was so superstitious that he canceled appointments scheduled on Friday the Thirteenth and wouldn't sit at tables of thirteen people.

Harry S. Truman
1945 to 1953

Before going into politics, Truman owned a men's clothing store.

Dwight David Eisenhower
1953 to 1961

This president was born David Dwight Eisenhower but decided to switch his first two names. Did he think it was an improvement?

John F. Kennedy
1961 to 1963

When making a speech in Germany, Kennedy meant to say "I am a citizen of Berlin" in German. He made a mistake. What he really said was "I am a jelly doughnut."

Lyndon B. Johnson
1963 to 1969

Johnson kept three television sets in the Oval Office. When he was president, there were only three networks, so he could keep his eye on every channel.

Richard M. Nixon
1969 to 1974

Richard Nixon was a good poker player. Despite his low army salary during World War II, he won enough from his games to finance his first campaign for Congress.

Gerald R. Ford
1974 to 1977

While studying law, Ford also worked as a fashion model.

James Carter Jr.
1977 to 1981

Jimmy Carter was the first president to be born in a hospital.

Ronald W. Reagan
1981 to 1989

Reagan lost some of his hearing, which may have been caused by the loud gunfire during all the Western movies he filmed in Hollywood.

George H. W. Bush
1989 to 1993

While he was campaigning for president, Bush was sometimes called a "wimp." Yet, he was a fighter pilot in World War II and flew fifty-eight combat missions.

William J. Clinton
1993 to 2001

Clinton has always been a book lover; he learned to read when he was three years old. He was also the first president to play the saxophone and to send an e-mail while in office.

George W. Bush
2001 to 2009

This President Bush was the first to hold Little League tryouts on the White House lawn. Perhaps it was no coincidence; years before, he was a managing partner of the Texas Rangers baseball team.

Barack H. Obama
2009 to 2017

One of Obama's favorite books is *Where the Wild Things Are*; he also has read all the Harry Potter novels. His high school nickname was O'Bomber because he was so good at basketball.

Donald J. Trump
2017 to ?

Donald Trump has a birthmark on both of his heels.

Glossary

Absentee ballot: a ballot that is marked and submitted in advance because a registered voter cannot get to the polls on Election Day

Amendment: a change in the wording or meaning of an existing bill or law

Ballot: a sheet of paper used to cast a vote

Bill of Rights: the first ten amendments to the U.S. Constitution; a statement of the basic rights and privileges of U.S. citizens

Campaign: the group of activities a candidate does to run for office

Candidate: a person who runs in an election for office

Chad: the bit of paper punched out of a ballot when a voter chooses a candidate

Congress: the national legislature of the United States, consisting of two sections, the Senate and the House of Representatives

Dark horse: a candidate whose talents and chances of winning are unknown

Delegate: a person who has the authority to act for others

Democracy: a government in which power is ultimately held by the people and used directly or through representation

Democratic Party: one of the two major political parties in the United States, organized in 1828, historically the party representing the interests of workers, minorities, and reformers

Dirty tricks: secret, unfair acts aimed at hurting the reputation or trustworthiness of an opponent

Election: the process of voting to choose a person for office

Elector: a member of the U.S. electoral college

Electoral college: a body of electors that elects the president and vice president of the United States

Executive branch: the section of the government that enforces the country's laws; it includes the president and all the agencies that report to the president

Founding Fathers: the people who help create a political institution. In the United States, the signers of the Declaration of Independence are often called the Founding Fathers, and those who created the Constitution are called Framers

Framers: the people who attended a convention in Philadelphia in 1787 to create the U.S. Constitution

House of Representatives: one house of the U.S. Congress, with 435 voting members (serving two-year terms); the number of representatives from each state is based on the state's population

Inauguration: the ceremony in which a new president takes office

Judicial branch: the court systems that interpret the country's laws and sometimes must decide if those laws obey the Constitution

Lame duck: an official who continues to hold office until the time when an elected successor takes over

Legislative branch: the section of the government that makes laws; the Congress

National convention: a meeting held every four years so a political party can choose its candidates for president and vice president and create its platform

Nomination: the act of proposing or choosing a candidate for office

Order of succession: the list of who gets the job if its current occupant resigns, dies, or is removed

Party boss: a leader in a political party who gains great power by controlling votes, political appointments, and favors

Platform: a statement of a political party's beliefs and goals

Political party: a group of people organized to get and use political power

Politician: a person who works in party politics or in the government

Polls: the place where voting occurs

Popular vote: the election results of the issues and candidates that ordinary citizens voted for

Primary election: an election that takes place within a party, before the national election, so that party's voters can express their choice of which candidates should run

Recount: a second count of votes when election results are in question

Republican Party: one of the two major political parties in the United States, organized in 1854, generally favoring business, a limited federal government, and strong national defense

Third party: a political party organized around interests different from those of the primary parties in a two-party system

Uncle Sam: the symbolic person who represents the U.S. government or the American people

U.S. Constitution: the document (including twenty-seven amendments) that defines the general framework for the U.S. government; the basic and ultimate law of the land

U.S. Senate: one house of the U.S. Congress, made up of two senators from each state, each serving a six-year term

Sources and Resources

There's a secret every nonfiction writer knows: research is fun. To get information for other books, I've paddled down the Amazon and used machines that trained astronauts to move in space. Talking to a few presidents for this book would have felt just as adventurous. Sadly, I encountered them only in books and on the Internet. Here are some books I used, most of which were written for grown-ups:

Boardman, Barrington. *Flappers, Bootleggers, "Typhoid Mary" & the Bomb: An Anecdotal History of the United States from 1923–1945.* New York: HarperCollins, 1989.

Boller Jr., Paul F. *Presidential Campaigns.* New York: Oxford University Press, 1996.

Brinkley, Alan, and Ted Widmer. *Campaigns: A Century of Presidential Races.* New York: DK Publishing, 2001.

Cook, Fred J. *American Political Bosses and Machines.* New York: Franklin Watts, 1973.

Dinkin, Robert J. *Election Day: A Documentary History.* Westport, CT: Greenwood Press, 2002.

Gumbel, Andrew. *Steal This Vote.* New York: Nation Books, 2005.

Mitchell, Jack. *How to Get Elected: An Anecdotal History of Mudslinging, Red-Baiting, Vote-Stealing and Dirty Tricks in American Politics.* New York: St. Martin's Press, 1992.

Smallwood, Frank. *The Other Candidates: Third Parties in Presidential Elections.* Hanover, NH: University Press of New England, 1983.

Tebbel, John, and Sarah Miles Watts. *The Press and the Presidency: From George Washington to Ronald Reagan.* New York: Oxford University Press, 1985.

Professional authors aren't the only ones who do research. You can too! There are a lot of ways to do it, starting with these nonfiction books:

Fritz, Jean. *Shh! We're Writing the Constitution.* New York: Penguin Young Readers Group, 1997.

Granfield, Linda. *America Votes: How Our President Is Elected.* Toronto: Kids Can Press, 2003.

Hoose, Phillip. *It's Our World Too! Young People Who Are Making a Difference, How They Do It—How You Can, Too!* New York: Farrar, Straus and Giroux, 2002.

Krull, Kathleen. *A Kid's Guide to America's Bill of Rights: Curfews, Censorship, and the 100-Pound Giant.* New York: HarperCollins, 1999.

Krull, Kathleen. *A Woman for President: The Story of Victoria Woodhull.* New York: Walker & Company, 2006.

Meltzer, Milton. *American Politics: How It Really Works.* New York: William Morrow and Company, 1989.

Timmesh, Catherine. *Madam President: The Extraordinary, True (and Evolving) Story of Women in Politics.* Boston: Houghton Mifflin Company, 2004.

Zinn, Howard, and Rebecca Stefoff. *A Young People's History of the United States*, volumes 1 and 2. New York: Seven Stories Press, 2007.

Fiction can be a great way to learn about history and the election process. Here are some novels to get you started:

Armstrong, Jennifer. *Thomas Jefferson: Letters from a Philadelphia Bookworm.* Part of the Dear Mr. President series. Delray Beach, FL: Winslowhouse International, 2003.

Bourne, Miriam Anne. *Nelly Curtis' Diary.* New York: Coward, McCann & Geoghegan, 1974.

Bradley, Kimberly Brubaker. *The President's Daughter.* New York: Delacorte Books for Young Readers, 2004.

Deutsch, Stacia, and Rhody Cohon. *Lincoln's Legacy.* New York: Aladdin Paperbacks, 2005.

Gutman, Dan. *The Kid Who Ran for President.* New York: Scholastic Paperbacks, 2000.

Rinaldi, Ann. *An Unlikely Friendship: A Novel of Mary Todd Lincoln and Elizabeth Keckley.* Orlando, FL: Harcourt, 2007.

Robinet, Harriette Gillem. *Washington City Is Burning.* New York: Atheneum Books, 1996.

Schmidt, Gary. *First Boy.* New York: Henry Holt & Company, 2005.

White, Ellen Emerson. *The President's Daughter.* The first book in the President's Daughter series. New York: Scholastic, 1994.

A different approach, all available on DVD:

All the President's Men (1976), a movie dramatizing the true story of two reporters who uncovered the Watergate scandal that led to President Nixon's resignation

Mr. Smith Goes to Washington (1939), a movie about an idealistic man who is appointed as a senator and confronts party bosses and corrupt politics

The West Wing (1999–2006), a TV show that portrayed the lives of a president and his staff through three elections and the years in between

Love the Internet? Start your research with these Web sites:

The Democracy Project: http://pbskids.org/democracy/

A guide to the electoral process: http://bensguide.gpo.gov/3-5/election/

All about the federal government: http://congressforkids.net/

Presidents: The Secret History: http://pbskids.org/wayback/prez/index.html

Here are Web sites about kids getting involved:

http://www.civicyouth.org/

http://www.whatkidscando.org/

Want to get involved yourself? Try:

http://pbskids.org/zoom/fromyou/elections/

http://sparkaction.org/act

Acknowledgments

As a politician once said, "It takes a village." I want to thank Bill Harris, Andrei Joseph, Denis Cleary, and Tracy Davies for the invaluable suggestions that got me started; countless curators at presidential libraries and government and voting organizations for clarification; the Library of Congress for its amazing documents and images; Dr. Ryan Lee Teten of Northern Kentucky University for sharing his work on kids and politics; and David Elliott, Deborah Hirschland, and Michael Roitman for their close reading and astute comments. Ron Wade and John Drayton generously lent us their campaign button collections. I'm lucky to work with Elwood Smith; I love his art, his droll sensibility, and his rep, Maggie Pickard. And I can't say enough about Donna Mark, Jennifer Healey, Sandy Smith, Melissa Kavonic, Beth Eller, Deb Shapiro, Eileen Pagan, and the rest of the people at Bloomsbury who helped bring this book into the world.

Finally, a special thanks to my editor, Jill Davis. She came up with the idea of an election book, then gave me every opportunity to make it my own. She has supported me and each opportunity to make the book better, even when it increased her load.

Picture Credits

Our democracy has borne many fruits, including our very amazing Library of Congress. Most of the photographs featured in *See How They Run* were obtained from its Prints and Photographs Division. The Library's collections contain more than 30 million cataloged books and other print materials in 470 languages; more than 58 million manuscripts; the largest rare book collection in North America, including a Gutenberg Bible; over one million United States government publications; one million issues of world newspapers spanning the past three centuries; 33,000 bound newspaper volumes; 5,000 microfilm reels; 4.8 million maps; 7 million sets of sheet music; and 2.7 million sound recordings.

The Library of Congress was created on April 24, 1800, by President John Adams when the government moved from Philadelphia to the new capital city of Washington. It was given $5,000 "for the purchase of such books as may be necessary for the use of Congress—and for putting up a suitable apartment for containing them therein."

The photographs on pages 8, 14, 18, 20, 22, 25, 37, 38, 45 (Abraham Lincoln), 47–48, 55, 57–58, 62–64, 68, 71, 83, and 85–88 (except George W. Bush and Donald J. Trump) are from the collection of the Library of Congress Prints and Photographs Division online at www.loc.gov. The remaining photographs were obtained from various sources. Page 6: Mt. Rushmore © Diademimages/ Dreamstime.com. Page 11: Statue © Pjc /Dreamstime.com. Pages 16, 29, 30, 34, 43: Courtesy of www.ronwadebuttons.com. Pages 24 and 59: Thomas Nast cartoons provided courtesy HarpWeek. Page 42: TV image © CBS/Landov. Pages 45 and 96: Elwood Smith courtesy of Joyce Ravid. Page 53: Voting machine courtesy of the Thomas Edison Papers at Rutgers University. Page 56: "Dewey Defeats Truman" © Bettman/Corbis. Page 70: George W. Bush © Iofoto/Dreamstime.com. Page 88: George W. Bush by White House photographer Eric Draper © Openstock Photography; Donald J. Trump by Jeff Kowalsky/AFP/Getty Images. Page 96: Susan Goodman courtesy of Michael J. Maloney.

Index

See Who Ran to Create This Book

Susan E. Goodman and **Elwood H. Smith** were the perfect team to write and illustrate *See How They Run*. They had already honed their partnership with *The Truth About Poop* and *Gee Whiz! It's All About Pee*. But more important they both have voted in every possible presidential election since they were old enough to register. Susan points out that Elwood has voted in many more elections than she has, but she hopes to make it up on the other end.

Susan's reason for voting: "It all depends on the election. Sometimes I vote for a candidate because I agree with his or her views. Other times it's because I hate everything one candidate stands for and want to do whatever I can to elect someone else."

And Elwood? "I love pulling that sideways lever; it simultaneously registers my vote and opens the curtains behind me! Sometimes I return disguised as a large water rat, just to watch that curtain fly open when other voters pull the lever. Large water rats are common where I live in the Hudson Valley."

To learn more about these singular citizens, visit their Web sites:

www.susangoodmanbooks.com
and
www.elwoodsmith.com